white-out

selected published poems
1986–2016

Saxby Pridmore

foreword by
Professor Tony Simoes da Silva

[Lacuna]
2016

Published in 2016 by Lacuna
http://www.lacunapublishing.com

Lacuna is an imprint of Golden Orb Creative
PO Box 185, Westgate NSW 2048, Australia
http://www.goldenorbcreative.com

© Saxby Pridmore 1986–2016

All rights reserved. No part of this publication may be reproduced, stored in a retrievals system, or transmitted in any form or by any means, electronic or mechanical, including photocopying, recording, scanning or otherwise, except under the terms of the Australian *Copyright Act 1969*, without the permission of the publisher.

All enquiries to the publisher: general@lacunapublishing.com

A National Library of Australia Cataloguing-in-Publication entry has been created for this title:

ISBN 9781922198242 (pbk)

ISBN 9781922198259 (ebook)

Cover and text design by Golden Orb Creative.
Poems typeset in 11/13.2 pt Palatino.

"Saxby Pridmore writes with clarity and total lack of pretension. The rich range of his poetry embraces humour and self-deflation, admiration of bravery and acts of mercy we doubt we could emulate, and rueful reflections on the ways we bend to regulations that demean our best impulses and noblest ideals. These poems consider everything human: the swamps and exhilarations of relationships, through childhood, working life and ageing. They're deft, poised, and compassionate. Many will stay in mind and invite revisiting the whole collection. It's good to see this poet's work so generously presented."

Michael Sharkey, editor of Australian Poetry Journal

"Saxby Pridmore's *White-out* explores the diversity of the personal and close at hand alongside coolly-observed, critical social commentary on the ills of the world. The collection offers passing nods to the gentle art of poetry, history, questions of science, and work-derived experiences from the field of psychiatry—with their explorations of the subways of the mind—within which Pridmore works, the writing being in turn perceptive, reflective, generous ..."

Ralph Wessman, former editor and publisher of Famous Reporter

"By turns whimsical and as penetrating as a surgeon's knife. From deeply personal to philosophically abstract, a powerful range of images and ideas."

Emeritus Professor James Cotton, UNSW Canberra

"Saxby Pridmore captures the feelings of any one of us—but in the melodic, poetic form we ordinary folk cannot master. From human relationships, so close we breathe them, to the wider world as seen from Tasmania and the Land Down Under, this collection is a surprise to enjoy."

Anne Henderson, author, biographer and deputy director of the Sydney Institute

"Professor Saxby Pridmore is the dedicatee of my first Piano Sonata, and was responsible for commissioning my second piano sonata 'Psychosonata'. Saxby's poem 'Kursk' inspired me to write, perform and record a piece of music by the same name. His beautiful poetry continues to inspire musical responses from me."

Michael Kieran Harvey, composer and concert pianist

Foreword

> The acquisition
> of armour
> by innocents, is growing up.
> *Saxby Pridmore, from 'Shelling' (p 130)*

In a series of poems spanning thirty years, Saxby Pridmore writes about some of the most basic levels of human experience in singularly meaningful and stimulating ways. Pridmore's *White-out* is a deceptively simple body of work that returns, time and again, to weighty themes such as life and death, living and dying. *White-out* combines serious writing, and serious thinking, and a mischievous sense of fun. Life as family, friends, places, relations of affect that criss-cross the everyday, longing and loss, all inflect the distinct worldview Pridmore captures in *White-out*. A poet and a scientist, a father, husband and friend, Pridmore offers in his poetry a series of snapshots of a moment, of an impression, of a memory. Each a self-contained unit, the poems combine to create a portrait of a life busily observing, reflecting, writing. Each in turn feeds into a richer narrative of being in and of the world, and of selfhood defined always relationally. The poems reflect an everyday wisdom tinged always by a wry sense of humour, occasionally veering on the cynical and disillusioned.

'There must be more to life than plenty', Pridmore writes in 'Us' (p 20). It is a sentiment that aptly conveys the mood of much of the writing included in *White-out*, the title of the book derived from its closing poem, 'What a time!' (p 182). It speaks of an underlying belief that the world is made richer through human interaction, through feelings, rather than the constant pursuit of material gratification. By 'plenty' Pridmore refers to the consumerist excesses of contemporary life, the insatiability of desire, the urge to do, to acquire, to accumulate just as quickly displaced by the boredom of satiety, the void engendered by a modernity made almost too ordinary as a result of the pervasive influence of technology. Elsewhere he writes that '[w]e all want things we haven't got' (p 72). By turns melancholic ('Caught on the hop', p 45) and exuberant—in 'The triple-jump in contemporary Australia' (p 162) he writes, in a moment of amused rapture, that it is '[t]ime to embrace the ballet of the streets'—political and meditative, Pridmore's writing journeys across time and experience, the speaking voice reflecting to varying degrees the weight of lived experience. Read as a body of work, it is easy to see a series of common themes and preferred techniques that enable the poet to articulate a distinct speaking voice.

The local informs Pridmore's vision but there is throughout an emphasis on a cosmopolitan sense of self, whether the tourist of 'Madrid 2004' (p 84), 'Venezia' (p 79) or 'Dachau' (p 76), or the engaged citizen of the world who wonders, repeatedly, 'Why we're dropping bombs on Bagdad?' ('Locked on', p 86). The use of the collective noun here is important for it speaks of a commitment to a responsible, ethical viewpoint that is present also in the poems that deal with contemporary Australia's historical and cultural legacy. In 'Kakadu' (p 51), for example, a poem ostensibly detailing a journey in the national park, Pridmore observes: 'We saw more crocodiles than aborigines. The people of the land / had left / (happily we were told) / their sacred sites and paintings / to be fenced and packaged / by whites / without dreaming.' The poem concludes: 'A proud, high stepping ancient lizard / unscathed by sun / or time or snake came out. / I slammed on the brakes too late. / It wasn't our fault.' The conflation of high-stepping lizard and Aboriginal people veers close to problematic but it is kept in check by the obviously political tone of the closing line—contemporary Australia continues to show limited interest in dealing with the legacy of colonisation and Aboriginal dispossession. Pridmore's quirky viewpoint, reflected in this poem but indeed one of the most salient aspects of his writing, often prevaricates and confounds, but each time a subtle and clever use of humour and irony deflates the sensitivity of a situation. Thus he writes, in 'Port Arthur' (p 75), of a constant tussle between white Australian historical memory and the erasure of Aboriginal culture: 'There's not much to see, really, at Port Arthur. Some sandstone ruins / of a couple of centuries / in a country / four hundred thousand centuries old.' A similar concern with the passing of a culture is reflected in 'The Awá People' (p 177), an Amazonian tribe whose first foray outside their forest world is met with the poisoned gifts of Coca-Cola and KFC. Yet this is by no means a conservative nostalgic viewpoint; 'What a time!' concludes with the line, 'I want to be buried in a 3D printed coffin', embracing, enthusiastically, the opportunities of the modern world.

Death, of a more personal nature, is a central theme in the collection. Invariably it is observed from a medical viewpoint, as inevitable and final, and in this sense it is at the heart of a distinctly secular vision. The poet's training and practice as a psychiatrist emerge in a concern with ageing and dementia, focusing on the death of the intimate self as much as on the physical self. 'Sagging' (p 104) speaks with brutal honesty of a suicide, and of the consequences for family and health officers. 'Coroner's delight' (p 114) returns to the theme: 'Another patient hung himself / in our ward today', the blunt assertion lightened up by the conclusion the speaker anticipates for the coroner's finding: 'With any luck / they'll blame the builder. / His distress should do. And / lucky us, he doesn't work here anymore.' 'Dad 1' (p 25) and 'Preparing for the River Styx' (p 31) bear witness to the ravages of death before it finally enacts its price, the suffering of the dying and of those awaiting their loved one's death rigorously detailed. Pridmore's poems often bring into relief the banality of death and dying, rather than its drama, and the discomfort of the infirm is set alongside the sorrow but also the impatience of those who will stay behind.

Yet, as the epigraph I start with illustrates, this collection is a celebration of life and living, of growing multiple 'selves' for different purposes and occasions. Identity is particularly centred on the family and the complexities of modern families, but also friends, acquaintances, roles and functions. Pridmore writes of the passage of time, both personal and collective. It is apt that the collection should offer a body of writing spanning three decades, for Saxby Pridmore's writing is best enjoyed as an assemblage of diverse works that coalesce to afford glimpses into a humane, and a humanist, sensibility.

Professor Tony Simoes da Silva
Head, School of Humanities
Faculty of Arts
University of Tasmania
May 2016

Contents

Foreword	v
About Saxby Pridmore	x
white-out **selected published poems, 1986–2016**	1
Index to poems	183
Index to publications	190

About Saxby Pridmore

Saxby Pridmore is an Australian poet living in Tasmania. Over the course of 30 years, he has had more than 300 poems published in over 40 different literary magazines and journals, including *Quadrant*, *Studio*, *Famous Reporter*, *Blue Dog*, *Overland* and *Island*. His poems have also appeared in anthologies, including: *Primary Care*, edited by Angela Belli and Jack Coulehan (University of Iowa Press, 2006); *Verbal Medicine*, edited by Tim Metcalf (Ginninderra Press, 2006); and *The Quadrant Book of Poetry 2001–2010*, edited by Les Murray (Quadrant Books, 2012). *White-out: selected published poems 1986–2016* is an anthology that brings together 194 of Saxby's published poems to commemorate his achievement and contribution to Australian poetry.

Saxby Pridmore is also a Professor of Psychiatry at the University of Tasmania, and has written several textbooks and over two hundred academic papers. He was made a Member of the Order of Australia for services to psychiatric treatment and research.

He and his wife Mary have a son and a daughter, and three grandchildren.

to Mary Elizabeth Pridmore

What there is

There is a yellow ball
under a bed
a topaz ring in a rusty tin
a grey glove on a gutter grate.

There is light all the time
darkness, all the time
time, all the time.

There is unconditional love
unconditional hate
there is combination loveandhate.

There are males, females and entrails

There is climbing mountains
reading books
and shooting civilians.

There is being certain
and uncertain
and not wondering.

There is being responsible
and irresponsible
there is wanting the thrill of a chance.

Contest runner-up, *Studio*, 2006

Limited edition

We struggled with your name
at first. Impotent
while you clung without nails
a limpet inside us.

Eighteen years down the track
you'll leave in love or anger
and the only thing you'll take
will be this name.

Quadrant, 1992

Day Two

I don't know what you
want.
We both cry.

In the end
a nurse brings a dummy
and you're contented
at first contact
with our culture of illusion.

Famous Reporter, 1993

Call to table
(for William)

Your mother's playing the piano
and Sesame Street is on

Schumann from the baby grand
Oscar from his garbage can

That rainbow spaghetti
life, is being served.

Centoria, 1998

Granny's place

Children with arms clamped to their sides
laugh over and over, rolling
down green garden slopes
to borders of cineraria and lily of the valley.

A dizzy swirl of wild roses, starlings
eucalypts and kids
all blessed by ancestral genes
to grow into the world and pass it on.

Wellspring, 2001

First teacher
(for Helen)

He asked, in his own way
but you had to know the language
long forgotten

and you had to know the way
yours and his
different but the same.

And you had to really listen
for it wasn't shouted out
for the question in his questions

nearly hidden by the gun
that he knew the secret secret
that not knowing is more fun.

You lifted up he looked
beyond our door
he saw

as you could.
He'll be
thankful for the listening and the lifting all his life.

Wellspring, 2001

Emma and the moth

She peeped into a tiny cage
of fingers
at a speckled moth.

"Let it go.
If the powder comes off
it can't fly."

It hobbled away in the air.
She beamed up from powdered hands,
"Now can I fly?"

Studio, 1987

Fish hooks

It's a design fault
that fish hooks cause fish pain.

It's not intrinsic to the aim
of putting molecules in men.

It's a design fault
like the pain of children leaving.

Home Brew, 1998

The fight of our lives

We fight
teeth and nails
tears for two.
No below the belt, OK?

We box on
bed and socks
TV then tea.
A dollar to be good?

A lucky punch
I go down
she rescues, "Daddy,
you're a mother to me."

Studio, 1993

Racing Emma

"Let's race to the car"
She quickened her step
but was drawn
to the toys in a window.

I forgot and
unlocked the door.

"You won by accident"
crystal tears
sucked up by
a thirsty dress.

In future
I'd try harder.

Studio, 1987

Child

He stands on the edge
of the end
of my life
– this boy of my middle years.

He plays with a toy
not knowing yet
what it is
– this boy who will care for his mother.

After a life spent
watching men
I know him
– by his struggling in my hands to be free.

Wellspring, 2001

For sale

Even as a boy
I wanted a boat-shed
a piece of paradise
I could lock for me.

At last one came up.
We got over beach and then rocks
ignored by the shrugging glass sea.
I twisted my knee.

Sagging years of neglect
bush growing through the floor
I was too late for this
And it was too late for me.

Emma's dog

"Emily's my sister," she said,
a huge woolly head on her lap.
A saddle-bag ear
flopped hand to hand
"I don't care,
if she came out queer."

Quadrant, 1992

The Boy's Own Annual

From day one, as though
from a dripping tap, seeping
into empty thinking cells
come stories of romance and regiment.
Bloody lies from Dumas and Kipling,
about a world that never was.

I push it all aside, too late,
and watch what I think, for life.

Visions, 1992

Taking down the Christmas tree

Twelve days after Christmas, about
the tree gives out
and it's time to take it down.

We chose you above all others
at the service station. You
were beautiful and green

tall, pyramidal, luxuriant
and you smelled of Christmas
excitement, long dead grandparents

childhood, puddings and presents.
And we dressed you in lights
angels, bells, baubles, tinsel, toy soldiers

and Father Christmases. Now
you're yellow and hard and
when I pull you out of the bucket

your needles, stiff as spears, sting
my hands. It's all you can do, to
get me back for financing your death

for using you, to pass on love
of Christmas to our children. Dying
for a good cause, you're in good company.

Weekend Australian, 1999

After asthma

Like a gymnast warming up, he coughs.

If I coughed half as hard, I'd do myself an injury
but his trunk is well prepared
and he goes into giant swings around the
    horizontal bar
with ease and doesn't wake.

Some drops of spit are fired out of slumber-swollen
    lips.
His chest of dragged-in air
as a crowd, squeezing past each other through the
    exit
whistles on escape, as he sleeps

he dreams stories he can tell.

Centoria, 1998

Gameboy

The latest Gameboy has two screens
One more than one can use
Or that's the way it seems
And extra buttons you can choose
A stylus thing for touching
For the impossible to be
For the hero to be leaping
In full colour and 3D.

Buy one for your son. Not for Christmas
Not for birthday, just for the hell of it.
Not for doing homework or turning up at mass
Just because you like to see the little fellow flip.
      Electrons might turn night into day
      But darling boys still love to play.

Studio, 2008

Father figure

You can't know
your father. Not as others
know him. By the time
she cared
there were only a few
years of him left.

Uncle Bill said he was
a marvellous man. Run
like the wind and as smart
as paint. And Auntie Ann said
he was so brave
when they took his wife away.

Childhood memories
of his crummy
boarding-school holidays
cooking. But she'd never gone
hungry. And he seemed
pleased she was happy

now. Maybe the hard years
had robbed him
of the power of speech. At least
about his heart.
She wished she'd known him
before she was born.

Mattoid, 1994

Shed fire

Son come shouting
"Shed's on fire"
I said, "It's all right mate,
it's a nightmare go back to …"
but with red reflecting everywhere
"No it's not!"

And there she was, Evil herself
red-yellow skirts swirling
arms in triumph clutching
at God's sky
sooled on
by the cannon banging of paint tins exploding
longing for the house.

Our hair crinkling short
we pitched
in with the garden hose
– she didn't even notice.

Till the fire boys got there
and took her out, their way.
She hissed
a bit

and spat black, sticky ash
that got walked into the carpet
and we loved the excitement.

Spindrift, 1998

Around the turn

I took a girl to play hockey
on Saturday and wandered over
to the track next door. It was
a golden day. The sun was bright
and hot in cloud-free blue,
the grass was green and smelt of being shaved,
the boys and girls were lean, brown gods.
It made me scared. I went around
the turn, around the turn, up
the straight, up the straight, around
the turn, around the turn, around
the turn – got my feet
and shoulders square on the home
straight, let my head go back. The
tape and officials and the crowd
had gone, thirty years ago. The grass
was mud, littered with dead, wet leaves.
Winter spiked my face and time is running fast.

Quadrant, 1993

Our psychotic cat

I think our cat's psychotic.
For no apparent reason
he leaps and runs
hissing
and sometimes, unexpectedly
he bites.

I catch him looking back –
he doubts me too.
He knows me as the one who
puts himself in water
eats fruit
and makes love face to face.

Studio, 1995

The old man

There was no away
from him.
For we were tied
not by cash or threat
but by those things
that still the tongues
and stop the fists of sons.

The post-Bradman years
were hard for him
where profit wasn't sin.
Where blisters were in history books
and regard for age
and elders was a curiosity.

We could wait, he wouldn't
be around forever
– but he was.
Then on his death
there was the guilt
of having wanted to be free.

Quadrant, 1994

Descending stairs

When he was at the top
you watched.
He was bloody good. Sure
of himself and strong
in command.

You didn't see his first step
down, more of a glide
and there he was
the same as ever. Above
the rest.

Most unexpectedly, he
came down another
one.
And it was sad
to see the grey.

He stumbled.
You steadied him.
You wouldn't have
years ago, but
something was wrong.

At the bottom step
he couldn't straighten up.
His hand was a fin of bone
in yours
and he didn't call you son.

Australasian Psychiatry, 1993

Dad

I visited the grave
of my father's brain, today
a bone sarcophagus
swathed in living skin.

The chest still pumps
to the legs, to carry it around
as if to find
a nice place for the planting.

Australasian Psychiatry, 1993

Us

Let us escape together
from this point and time.

There's food in the cupboard
just toss some in a back-pack

and let's go together.
There must be more to life than plenty.

Quadrant, 2014

Out walking

There you were
straggling along behind the family
a little kid with hat
and bag that were too big.

I dropped back
to keep you company.
But soon, you wondered
what made the others laugh
and caught them up

leaving me
in your place.
Behind, alone, too frail to close the gap.

FreeXpresSion, 2001

Grandma

She goes, when she's got the time.
She has to make time, on birthdays
and then she's got to do the rounds
in case one feels left out.
If she hasn't got the time
she doesn't go – it can be hard to get away.

There's wall flowers for her father
he always liked that
and pansies for the twins, who never breathed.
Rosemary for remembrance, for Wal
and a rhododendron for him too
from the first plant he ever gave her.
Solomon's seal for her mother
– she always had it in her gardens.
And Veronica for love, they all get a bit of that.

New England Review, 1997

Saving Grandma's walker

You could eat the smoke when we arrived
a yellow tiara flickered on the hill
as we tunnelled into a wind from Hell.

We turned the car and scooped her up
with nighties, pills, and a built-up shoe
then lash clicked her seat-belt safely.

But our rush and tumbling stopped
"I'm not going without my walker," she said.
But, Granny we can get you another one!

"No. I'd be a nuisance without my walker."
One ran like a hero saving a singed-hair child
with red embers falling as Satanic snow.

Then down the winding hills we drove
"Thank you for getting it, my dears," she said
"I'd have been a nuisance without my walker."

Idiom, 2014

Cordless in Mexico

Not a word in six months
the cordless phone comes
hand to mouth
I wonder what on earth to say.

Hello Dad
Just to let you know
I'm in Mexico.
The coins are running out, she has to go.

I didn't know you left Australia. Click.

And so, she still has speech
the ability to ring
and go where I have never been.

Quadrant, 2001

Dad 1

Death, a fickle girl
wanders from room to
room in my father's
brain, sucking bits
and spitting them back
out. A choosy tenant
in a buyer's market coming back
for a second and third
look, and never making up her mind –
just scrimmaging through skeletons'
cupboards, blowing dust off
stacks of worn memories. We wait stiffly
for her to slam the door and take the lot.

Imago, 1994

Noel (3)

It had to come
but it was still a shock
a laden coffin
being lowered into me

pressing on my breast bone
heavier and harder
till my ribs would snap
but getting through

pushing lungs
and heart aside
still back and down
to splinter

into wooden stakes
on contact with my spine.

You can't keep
a good man down
and I go off to vomit up your death.

Quadrant, 1994

Noel (4)

You died the way
men from the back blocks
used to do.
No carry on, just died.

We didn't think to ask
just put you in the ground.
No speeches, just a hole.

You would've said yourself
in ten years' time
the only ones who'll know
'll be the ones
who dug the bloody thing.

Quadrant, 1994

NX5331

He's dead now.
His grandson (my son)
's got his medals.

His mob lobbed at Suez
and they were slogging
from Palestine to Egypt, when he copped it

and fought a war
for the rest of his life, with his nerves
his back and his gammy leg.

(My boy's got his hatband and his pocket-knife
as well.) But the poor old bugger
never told us much. Except

from time to time, desert names
including Tel Aviv and Bethlehem
Gaza, Haifa and Jerusalem; in a way that

they were home.
We've given to the war effort
– my boy's Grand-dad went for him.

Past the Poppies, 1996

Frail

Deep, back behind your throat
is a long drop, and
at the bottom
on the diaphragm
is the pool of sadness.

And as you go about your day
now, the kids are off your hands
life is about
keeping the pool as calm as a saucer of milk

about not having
a fragment fall
down
in slow motion
down and down
to smack into the pool
and send ripples of sadness
out, to the edge of your existence.

You can't take that anymore.

You can't take it, when a piece of something gets away
and you feel it fall
all the way down
and the impact
and the sadness going sideways, out
then down your arms and legs.

You focus on the grand-kids, and check they've had
    their shots.

Quadrant, 2003

Living comet

She was born before I met
her mother, but
we were father–daughter
for twelve years.

The big bang of divorce
sent her into yet another orbit.
As a comet she comes round
once in many years.

She's just been past, close
enough to touch
and timid talk. We circle
round and peck upon the corpse.

Then she orbits off
to a life-sustaining planet
somewhere secret in the universe, where
the shock waves of big bangs never reach.

Quadrant, 2002

Preparing for the River Styx

It would be a waste to over-pack
she only needs one case.

Like Hillary and Tenzing
she's been in training all her life, and
the travel agents down the church
have given her a map.

We can locate a coin for Charon
when that time comes
– for the moment we're just sitting
saying what we can

the word courage has not come up
– we are grateful for her faith.

Famous Reporter, 2000

Informed consent

How did they get Dad's ashes
as fine as face powder and uniform light grey?

His organs, liver
spleen and pancreas
wrapped in fat, may have burned to grey
– but his backbone would have made
a little row of brittle black blocks.

They must have swept
his elbows and ankles, all his bone coals
into some big grinder, set to the finest size.

He would have much preferred
(we didn't think to ask about our options)
to go through a sieve
for old times' sake
for all the concrete floors and foundations
paths and steps he made, every place we lived
with a hand-held sieve
strong arms jerking
side to side – one of cement to three of sand
mixed with gravel
with a scraping shovel
worked into a walled dam
to hold the water from a watering can.

Depending on the combination, sand
pure silica white through to nearly black
and brand of cement
came the colour of the concrete. When
fully dried, he often got the colour of his ashes.

We didn't know to say
we would have liked his grain less prissy.
About as coarse as The Fisheries beach
would have been the thing. Something
you could feel but that didn't
lubricate your finger tips, like he does now.

Why did they make him
uniform grey?
Did they think we wouldn't want
to know
his hip bone from his ear?

This was not a bland man.

Probably, it all comes down to storage space
– to get a man that size, into a jar this size
you'd have to get his molecules to lie
pretty close together
and fine grinding is possibly
the only way to go.

We should bury Mum
(when she's dead of course).
I hear they put pink dye in for girls
– just joking. But
he wasn't like
other men, when he was alive
it's a shame to make him like them now he's dead.

Muse, 2002

Winter

You know it's winter
when you hold your water
when you won't touch your dick
with your icicle fingers
and you stand in the park
for the dew on the benches
is too thick to sit.

And the old houses are going
as the forts are coming
with fences you can't see over
finished like dining room tables
and seamless garages
with anti-graffiti non-stick sides
and hidden locks.

They cut the footpath up
and patched it back
with yellow plastic flaps for "GAS"
and a shag stands on a slip-yard rail
that continues to rust.
You know it's winter when
you haven't seen your child in years.

Famous Reporter, 2006

Harrington Richardson

Thunder from his gun
Sent a leaping hare
Spinning in the air.

He broke it. Smoke wisp with
The sting of fire-crackers
And lob-bobbed a new load in.

There was no knife.
Sandpaper fingers
Ripped the skin and belly open.

Holding the head and back legs
A single wobble-board flick sent
The guts into the grass.

He pushed one ear up inside his belt
And knotted them on top.
Now there was one each side.

He had them facing out, so
His trousers wouldn't get grubby.
He was your grandfather.

Quadrant, 2014

Split second

It set off
the billowing
atom bomb of justice
which made things so much worse

with the newspapers
and their public, their 'right to know'
their need to see justice being done
or, more likely, wanting a bloody good perve.

Of course, it wouldn't happen
if he had his time again, he
just lost control.
It must have been the piss.

He remembers thinking
to be careful
as he got the gun down
because he only meant to frighten

her. He remembers the kick
and the splatter.
A one-way valve clicked
God ignored his pleading

and he couldn't have 'slips'.
It was an accident, a stupid split
second, that killed them all
in a way. It must have been the piss.

Quadrant, 1995

Love

I'm a mirror
image of the lady
who can't say 'fuck'
in court.

I'm the man
who can't say 'love'
in you

and has to write it down.

Quadrant, 1992

Migraine

I'd have it for you
– the spear in the eye.

With grey lips and vomit
running from your nostrils
a spear goes through my heart
– better in my eye.

Quadrant, 1996

Thanks for the extra arm

When you left
to find your course
I had to save myself.

That achieved, your phone call
returned the arm
you took, inadvertently.

Severed by the sharp
edge of the top
it fell inside your case.

I grew another
not perfect, but good enough for most things.
I'm like a dog with two tails.

Broad Seat, 2001

The Hiroshima of divorce

From the Hiroshima of divorce
blind mice who once were men
sound out one another
with echoes in the head
and sniff out every nook for love
for time alone won't heal.

It begins in lace
near a happy ending
they grow together
then tear apart
leaving bleeding pieces
in the company of one.

Scabs peel like confetti
scars fade in the sun
but on white sticks
drawn to the warm
they burn again
the cure is the cause.

Brave New Word, 1988

Yellow dress

Close on the steps
her yellow dress pressed
gift-wrapping her body
a tug away.
Her single-handed waist
sharp-edged mouth
and creases of her smile
squeeze the sticky taste of lust
into his mouth.
All else is gone
instinct locked in
he pushes silly words
through a deadpan face.
The feast of a lifetime
her covered flesh
to grab and bite
and pick her up
and make her love with him.
Forcing fingers into fists
he backs down
and says 'goodnight'
for another night.

Brave New Word, 1988

Her rings

He was handsome and unfaithful.
When his affairs ended
he brought her a new eternity ring.
She had an engagement ring
a wedding ring
and three eternity rings.

She found another perfumed handkerchief
removed her rings
took down his antique muzzle-loader
poured powder down the barrel
rammed home the wadding handkerchief
to hold the charge
and dropped the rings on top.

He came home
late and smiling.
At point blank range
she fired her rings into his heart
and his mother's blackened handkerchief
fluttered down upon his chest.

Edgeways, 1988

Poem to a woman

Need I
like you
to hold.

Had it all
fucked it up
it fucked up
fucked me up.

Now football knees
my boozer's gut
the wife's vasectomy
have made me old.

Leave naught
to trade
for love but need.

Writing, 1990

Life's work

What's left is yours,
this fag-end of a worked life
beaten out, folded over
and beaten out again.

Take it
I owe it to you.
Guilt by virtue
of age. In the older man
honoured by a younger wife.
Go on,
it's the least I can do.

It's the best I can do.

Still,
I could use any
you don't need.

Studio, 1995

Going overboard

You go overboard,
She said
You can't relax.
You're a slave
to responsibility.
It's making you a bore.
They'll take care of your kid
just fine
and don't forget
my birthday
or Christmas
and ring me if you're late.

Brave New Word, 1988

Caught on the hop

You came into my house, unannounced.
We talked of school days
our second marriages, then
it got around to what we had been doing lately.

Without warning, you pulled up your shirt
to show
where they cut you in half to put in
the lungs of a teenage boy.

I was angry with you for frightening me
for being the centre of attention
for doing something I'd never done
for the teenage boy.

You should have given me warning.
We hadn't been introduced. Suddenly
there was a strange
pair of lungs bellowing in my living room

with you, grinning
between immuno-suppressed cheeks.
I didn't want you to cough or spit
I didn't want to breathe your expelled air.

I didn't know whose lungs you had
or how his family felt about you being there.
I am an average man
ashamed of not being good with the unfamiliar.

Studio, 1998

The counsellor is coming

She's determined not to drink
again. Good kind
mother and wife.

He's determined not to gamble
again. Well meaning
penniless dad.

The problem is they've
got problems.
So the counsellor is coming

to adjust their genes, knit
them new childhoods
and compensate with soothing

for their stillborn twins.

The Mozzie, 2005

Reel

Of course he loves his wife and kids
and wants the best for them. Of course
he'd give them anything he could. But
he's a bit short this week
so could she borrow twenty bucks
from her mum so they can eat.

At the dice toss of conception
the fly fishermen of genes
cast a hook of many molecules
that caught a lever of his soul.

How he hates the pokies
and the bastards who invented them
the hotels that parade them
and the politicians, who look the other way.

And of course he has free will, and of course
he makes his choices, about
coffee, black or white and the colour of his tie.
But as his car drives past the pokies

it has free will too
it turns into the parking lot
and turns its engine off.
He sits, hands on the wheel.
He feels the clicking of the reel
the fly fisherman of genes leans back and pulls a
    lever of his soul.

The Mozzie, 2007

Bradman played cricket

I'm a mechanical adding machine
with a rusty arm, for cranking down
to spin the gears
inside your guts.

Dust has collected, thick
black and sticky, where
the oil used to be put in.

I've been superseded
by a lighter
faster
cleverer
cheaper
Dick
Smith
Hong
Kong
electronic chip
without a moving part.

I can't interface with email.
I'm pre-decimal currency, mate
carbon paper and Bradman were my
       contemporaries.

No, Carbon Paper didn't win the Melbourne Cup!
That was Carbine.
Bradman? He played cricket.

The Mozzie, 2006

Mary

Her sick mother was taken away
Leaving housework not dolls to play
    And boarding school at the age of eight
    Shaped hair and clothes into out of date

Mother's letters were the single link
And what she wrote was the single chink
    For love to drop through down
    To a little girl who was lost and found

By her God Mother who had her own brood
Who kissed her hair and found enough food
    Weekends away from boarding-school strife
    Were the other portal to a well-loved life.

Her father of five loved all he could
He didn't know dancing but he did know God
    She was roughly ready for the world
    Into which she strode as it unfurled.

She painted on canvas, girls and their mothers
And made room in her life for generous others
    The gem polisher tumbled her around
    When she emerged, no flaw was found.

She married once and a good boy flowed
And now to the end of my silly ode
    To my saviour wife
    Who watered my life.

Idiom, 2016

The Story of the Bead People

When they came they brought
Glass beads
Red and green
Gaudy, bright and dazzling
To quell the people of the land.

And it worked extremely well.
So every New Year's Eve
They celebrate
With a big corroboree
And throw a bag of beads across the sky.

Famous Reporter, 2002

Kakadu

In Kakadu
we saw more crocodiles
than aborigines.
The people of the land
had left
(happily, so we were told)
their sacred sites and paintings
to be fenced and packaged
by whites
without dreaming.

One day two came up
as black as your hat
drunk, slurred
coughing, scarred and stinking.
We drove to get away
foot to the floor.

A proud, high stepping
ancient lizard
unscathed by sun
or time or snake came out.
I slammed on the brakes
too late.
It wasn't our fault.

Fremantle Arts Review, 1991

The people of the *Batavia*

The *Batavia*, pride of the East
India Company
dressed from spritsail to mizzen
ran aground and broke on Morning Reef.

Hundreds were stranded
on the atolls of Houtman Abrolhos
with no shelter or water
only chests of Company treasure.

When the captain went for help, hell
flew open, a mother and daughters
were murdered, along with many men
and they gouged out the eyes of a boy.

Salvation arrived on the *Zaandam*.
The hands of seven guilty were hacked
off before they were hanged
keelhauling for others.

Wouter Loos and Pelgrom de By
were marooned on mainland Australia.

Back in Java, the retribution continued
– they broke the back and every bone
of Jacob Pieterz, twisted his limbs
till his bones came through the skin
and tied him, contorted, to a cart wheel.

After more amputations, hangings
brandings and whippings
justice was finally done. Strangely
all survivors lived short, sad lives.

But what of Loos and Pelgrom de By
the first white men to live on Australia?
Perhaps they ate low-cholesterol snake
and drank fresh spring water
made friends with the aborigines
and died old, happy
to have escaped the well and civilisation.

Imago, 1998

Ludwig II

Ludwig
was king
of the castle

he built
Neuschwanstein
– emblem of Disneyland.

Insane
he was kept
in cold Berg Castle. He

took his doctor
by the throat
and drowned them both, in

Starnberger Lake. Tourists
tremble at the tragedy
of the sad 'Mad King of Bavaria'

– what about his doctor's children?

Australasian Psychiatry, 1997

Mentioned in dispatches

No Marcel Caux on Anzac Day.
For eight decades and four, he wouldn't talk.
Silence kept the men he killed away.

At the silent movies he would play
his cello, sitting down. One leg wouldn't walk.
No Marcel Caux on Anzac Day.

He went farming, planting, cutting hay.
His gun with bayonet became a fork.
Silence kept the men he killed away.

Carpentry, when 'talkies' came to stay
dead trees to shape, not men to turn to chalk.
No Marcel Caux on Anzac Day.

Eventually the children said, they would like to say
the family had a hero, and he shouldn't baulk.
And, silence hadn't kept the men he killed away.

The prattle press have had their way
with man of Somme, whom spectres stalk
who wouldn't march on Anzac Day
for silence kept the men he killed away.

The Mozzie, 2005

Kaesong River, 1952

He found
the bandy little bugger
on the other bank
in his telescopic sight.

God knows why
he waited for him
stumbling from sleep
to kneel at the frozen edge.

Lowering his killing cross
to the chest
he held it there
afraid to breathe a cloud. Till

the fellow on the other side
splashed icy water on his face
and never knew
what took his breath away.

Forty years on
a sniper died
dreaming of Korea
and got what he deserved.

Westerly, 1992

The Hon. R. A. Pargiter

A brass microscope of a man
tarnished by the sweaty hands
of others over time
he stands singular
inviting us to peer
through him, at the world he sees.

A wooden dinghy of a man
cracked and crusted
but sea worthy
tugging at his moorings
still inviting with the vigour
of his first day in the water.

As the Jack's furled
the question comes
is this the kind we're leaving?
The answer, No
his kind has no single land
and rarely comes from anywhere.

Australasian Psychiatry, 1993

1965

If I could have one year again
it would be 1965.

We railed against sending men
to kill in Vietnam

And railed against sending men
to die in Vietnam.

We railed against the Springboks
For being white

And in blacked-up faces clogged up
the airport lounge.

Dawn was barred for winning excessive
Medals in swimming

[If you can't beat 'em, don't let 'em
Play.]

Our golfing Peter won the British Open
Yet again and

Roma M got over the men as the first
Female beak.

All in my first year down in Brisbane
From the bush.

And best of all the 'Shrimp'* from
Blighty went to the Flemington races
With a hem four inches up her thigh
No stockings and wearing a man's watch.

* British model Jean Shrimpton

Idiom, 2016

Hawley Beach 1

Twice a day
the sea pulls back

and we steal oysters
over the rocks.

We know her tricks
and never let her get around behind.

She throws waves and smiles in wait
beyond the sight of land.

Mattoid, 1994

Snails

Overnight rain brings snails
feeling out across the path
before the sun. A tiny one
with a shell like baby's fingernail
stands off to windward
from a tortoise shelled mother.

They sail together
overland
Heemskirk and Zeehan
for the Great South Land
in a light breeze
with a silver paper wake.

Vibrations in the ground
alarm. No speed.
They hatch down
in spiral bunkers
– no match
for the joggers beating death.

Redoubt, 1998

The brave tram driver

In April 1960
Ray Donoghue's tram
lost its brakes
on the decline into Hobart.

He could have jumped
or gone up the back and braced
himself.
But he stayed at his controls
and dinged the bell

across the
Patrick
Brisbane
Melville
Bathurst
Liverpool
and Collins Street
intersections

and smashed full speed
into the stationary tram at the terminus.

God knows
how many lives he saved
with his terror bell. He got The George Cross
posthumously, but they never made the movie.

Quadrant, 2000

On the Maria Island ferry

On the way home, through drizzle
we cuddled in the ferry belly
under our condensing breath. Till

from grey stipple
curved needles flashed
out and in – dolphins
silver crescents racing
to port and starboard, ahead
astern and pacing by our side.

We stood up
bubbles tickled in our legs
expanded in our chests and came cheering out.

Lexicon, 1997

Demolition of the Battery Point boat sheds

Thirsty boards that hadn't seen a lick
of paint since the coronation
off-square doors, lost-key padlocks
thistles growing through the floor, toward
    sun-stars
in flapping tin roofs. Rusting
chain, ends of heavy, greasy rope
paint brush bristles stuck together
stiff as handles

all pushed into piles of cobwebbed planks
warped ply', dented drums
barnacled posts, barbed wire, beer bottles
with silverfished labels, franger packets
bent nails and one brass screw.

Their demolition was front page news
but
they were deserted long ago, for the marina
by those who loved them.
The shrugging waves
care even less and know the world's not flat.

Gathering Force, 1997

McGrath

There'll be no 'Back to Borneo'
trip, for 'The Human Colander'
of Tarakan.

Twenty days to the surrender
he and his mate got whacked
by a booby trap, on Snaggs Track.

His mate got a single piece
in the middle of the chest
and died where he landed

while our bloke went to wipe
the blood from his face and found
floppy sausages for fingers.

And more had gone
through the nerves of his legs
into his belly and back.

They took him to Morotai
tried this 'penicillin' as a gesture
and blow me down, he lived.

His hand doesn't respond
to 'Back to Borneo' ads. He
left something there he doesn't need.

Past the Poppies, 1996

Manneken Pis

In Brussels, the great attraction
is a bronze of a boy having a leak.
He's not in any art books
there is no claim of artistic qualities.

Naked, life size
he stands high
on a wall at a cobbled corner
and has since sixteen something.

Shock cannot
withstand familiarity.
His fame depends on an endless flow
of those who want to see, a boy going to the toilet.

Broad Seat, 2001

Before hockey

Balls of dew on blades of grass
and white pin feathers, thrill
in the cold
of an early game morning.

Famous Reporter, 1997

On a jetty

A mountain backs Hobart
blinking
pastelled in by early light
as a duck swims
at a pyramid point
over an estuary starfish.

Time is sliced
and frozen
and we are blessed and damned.

Famous Reporter, 1997

Laurens Koster

For the words
you are about to receive
thank Johannes Gutenberg

of Mainz, father of the printing press
famous for inventing
the medium of fame.

But the Dutch
claim Laurens Koster
came first and took the book to Mainz.

With European unity, Koster
embedded in a national pride
will glide. The accountants are changing history.

Studio, 2005

Hawley Beach 2

The rustling early sea
hides voices
of the dead.
Rocks come and go
across the spit,
boobyalla and ti-tree
crowd us down
to the middens
of before. Black phantoms
push me back
to the cold coffin
of a windowed room.
And I watch
till sun
on sand
starts time again.

Mattoid, 1994

Thinking on death

No one knows why Amschel Rothschild
hanged himself
– he owned a vintage Maserati
and a biplane.

As he walked on air he felt a foot kick
the chair over
– so he knew, there was no way back
from the jig.

What were the thoughts he chose?
no one knows
– there was his mother with a compress
during chicken pox.

No time to lose, father's face, Auntie Grace
the smell of wife
– the golf day with the Board when he went
in the bunker.

He maybe nearly panicked, to get it right
one more time
– or perhaps he sang to that welcome twang
a first song

of defiance
– and refused to think of anything at all.

Spindrift, 1999

Driving to Craigie Knowe Vineyard

The sky is royal blue
and around the waterfront
– electric lights are weak
without the night to push against.

We drive across the dappled, grey river
striped by spars
from street light stars.

Now pastel clouds
– rice paper screens
slide over one another.
They expose (momentarily)
the moon, a bone-white ghost
and a pink lipstick line
is drawn across behind the coming hills.

Cottages and the bodies of dead gums
stand
ancient
etched
delicate as fossil fish
and the clouds close.

The angry locked out sun
stamps
opal
into
the canopy
and the day begins to tick
as we turn
in and drive along the vines.

Studio, 1999

Back home

You've got a problem when
you've only brought designer shoes
and the dew's so thick
you can't step off the path

and the parrots make
such a din
you can't hear the spilling creek
you can remember.

They take off
sweeping Joseph's cloak
across leaning, mossy trunks.
Hidden

under filtering man-fern fronds
is the quiet before history.
I stoop in.
I look down and my feet are wet.

Centoria, 1999

Queenstown, Tasmania

Everybody's inside, asleep
in the cold fog
in the early morning.

Most of the pubs shut down
no-one to buy the beer
the banks, no-one to borrow.

The Presbyterian Church
turned into a Gallery
on the way to going broke.

There's an Ex-servicemen's Club
a cenotaph with a field gun
and the War Memorial Hall.

At last a boy goes by on a bike.
Still the town waits
for the promised reconstruction

and the steam train buffs
to bring back prosperity.
We all want things we haven't got.

Quadrant, 2000

Bronte Hydro Village

Cocoon quiet
mornings. White
frost with bellows breath
from the core into the cold
that could snap a bone
from slip on ice on stone.

We stayed two days
where they had lived
– the migrants who built
the Hydro dams, high
for our convenience
– we, perched below by beach.

We pack to get back down
to avoid
thinking of their chilblains
of hands caught in machinery
– all aglow
with fashion-conscious guilt.

Older now
on low land plots, they
hold memories
– of drinking lots of happy juice
playing poker
and being pleased to have a job.

Core, 2000

How television saved the world*

Yes, we took some cash that wasn't ours
not big money, like in white collar crime
and yes, we may have scared a few rich folks
in banks, tending to their fortunes. But
don't forget, in our ransom note for Patty
we demanded food and clothing for the poor.

This in the time of Vietnam and Watergate
– others had snatched John Paul Getty three
and sent his right ear to his dad
in the post. And we didn't lie like Nixon did.

That was on a distant planet, in another time
I was a different person then, so was everybody
    else
and so it would have stayed
but for human nature – the greed of television
    captains
their husbandry of those too lazy for a life
catering for curiosity and blood lust, without any of
    the risks.

---

* Kathleen Soliah was captured after an
  episode of "America's Most Wanted".

Studio, 2001

Port Arthur
(for Dag Aarsland*)

There's not much to see, really
at Port Arthur. Some sandstone ruins
of a couple of centuries
in a country
four hundred thousand centuries old.

Souvenirs, of the evil hand of man
dozing
not extinct (see Bosnia).

---

* Written for an overseas visitor twelve months
before the massacre.

Studio, 2001

Dachau

We had a lovely day
at Dachau.
They'd let the place run down
but luckily, before too late
they saved the best bits.

The crematorium
that got too small
the bigger one
outside the wall.
The shower room
with poison gas, they said
had never been turned on.
The strip of grass
next to the fence
where you could run
if you wanted to be shot.

It was an education.
It was good we got
a sunny day
in rain
it could have been quite drab.

Broad Seat, 2001

Kursk

We only have one torch
We are keeping it turned off
Most of the time.

We are lying on top bunks
We have the air in front of us
Our backs against the Barents Sea.

We have children in Murmansk.
We are in a metal case
On the ice floor.

We only have one torch
We are keeping it turned off
Most of the time.

We are living up our oxygen.
We felt the piss of terror first
But we are over that.

We have faithful wives waiting.
We only hope
The batteries don't run out.

We only have one torch
We don't want to die
In the dark.

Quadrant, 2006

The Centre Pompidou

looks like Disneyland dropped an oil
refinery in the middle of Paris.
It has coloured tubes and passages all over
the outside (you can't see out the windows).
Blue for air-conditioning, yellow for electricity
green for water and red for people.

It houses the Bibliothèque Publique d'Information,
 but
they refuse to host wood-chopping championships.
It has the Institute de Recherche et Co-ordination
 Acoustic/
Musique, but they say *non* to roof-top clay pigeon
 shoots.
It has the Musée National d'Art Moderne, but
won't permit sheep-dog trials on the piazza
 outside.

The Centre Pompidou is a partial success; showing
colour coding works, but at the cost of multi-
 functioning.

Quadrant, 2016

Venezia

We saw the beauty of the buildings
the awkward gondolas, forced to work
the Titians and Tintorettos of Accademia
and St Marco's Basilica and piazza
with pigeons, really topped it off.

We told ourselves and others that the dereliction
of the palaces along the Grand Canal, added
to their majesty.
We'd spent good money getting there
we'd rather lie than waste it with the truth.

Sad city of mask and glass, of history and art
of light and architecture. Now
façades missing and shutters shut but sagging
deserted by old families for convenience.
Crawling with tourists who won't admit they're on
      a corpse.

We walk our son from one site of exploitation
across Scalzi bridge to another square
– he liked the pigeons best.
City with no trees
he'll need to come when he's big, to find Australia.

Sidewalk, 2002

Victoria*

If we had the money
we'd take her body back.
But working people can't afford
the luxuries of death.

She'll have to stay
where her killer lives.
We must go home to Rome
and leave her body here.

With flesh gauged off her skull
as purple orange peel
we'll cover her in satin, first
and leave her body here.

The body's here
the girl is gone
her sisters still need things

we'll go, and leave her body here.

* An Italian tourist, murdered on an Australian beach.

Muse, 2002

The McCord Museum

Cradleboards and snow-shoes
wampum strings and
Mr Trudeau's pin-stripe suit
hang together
in McCord Museum, Montreal.

Things
looked after on condition
that we can touch the past.

They bring us
pre-penicillin children
and the pre-black pain of frozen feet.

We hurry on
to Mr Trudeau's suit
and pretend he had it easy.

Quadrant, 2003

The Pinnacles
(Nambung National Park)

They
stand
on golden
sand
but
are not
grand.
Like nudes
they're better
in pictures.
Curiosities
dumb freaks
Rorschach
shapes
you read
your life into.

Quadrant, 2005

Cradle Mountain and surrounds

We stayed three days
at Cradle Mountain, shaped
by scraping glaciers
of the last ice age.

We walked around Dove Lake
on duck boards and dolerite
and tripping white quartzite
through the Ballroom Forest, respectfully

to Pencil Pine Creek where
yellow-eyed currawongs
stole the food we chewed
and echidnas didn't want to get involved.

From Wombat Pool amid pin-cushion plants, up
to Crater Lake and wallabies
with rosellas and honeyeaters in deciduous beech
up, past Lake Lilla and King Billy Pine, up

from Wombat Peak to Marion's Lookout
where you can see your life spread out
like a map on a war-room table. I made it
before I was too old, to see what I had missed.

The Mozzie, 2005

Madrid 2004

Velazquez was here. And Picasso
Goya, the Moors and Columbus
the flamenco, Dali, El Greco
the bullfights. Then Guernica

lawyers, plumbers and tailors
on their way to work or shopping
were blown to bits of bone
with meat attached
eyes rolling
on platforms like marbles
as handfuls of fingers
flew through the air
some with dirt under nails.

Their mobile phones kept ringing
calls to the dead not getting through
there is something here to bury
and humanity needs digging up.

Blue Dog, 2005

Firdo Square

It was a fine day
but a bit too much
looting. In the evening
for a lark, we put the flag
over your face
and pulled your statue down.

You showed no respect
so we towed
your empty head
around the streets.
We came
to Firdo Square to set a good example.

The Mozzie, 2005

Locked on

Can you tell me once again
Why we're dropping bombs on Bagdad?
With pictures of the place aflame
Just tell me once again
Was it Saddam who was bad?
Can you please explain again
Why we're dropping bombs on Bagdad?

The Mozzie, 2005

Work

Joseph of Arimathea might
have got some feedback
on the fellow's thinking
as he hammered
spikes through Jesus' hands
down, down, down, into the wood

as far as the Christian soldiers
of Abu Ghraib prison are
concerned, it was nothing
personal, they didn't even know those guys.

Studio, 2007

Ali Abbas

Mohammed, Matti, Azhar and Abeer
gave me a bike on my birthday
and I hugged each one in tears.

I grabbed it from their cheers
and raced it out to play
Mohammed, Matti, Azhar and Abeer.

The best news I could hear
was they were there to stay
and I hugged each one in tears.

Each one to me was dear
my family bouquet
Mohammed, Matti, Azhar and Abeer.

Back before I knew the fear
of Bagdad blown to clay
and I hugged each one in tears.

Back before the missile that tore
my arms away
killed Mohammed, Matti, Azhar and Abeer.

Now I can't hug but I still have tears.

published as "Inside Ali Abbas", *The Mozzie*, 2007

Walking near Mt Fuji

On every path you come across
clustered gods
sanded back
almost to starting stone.

Even gods cannot resist
the weather over time
and even ten put in a ring
get no respect from moss.

Stubbled statues hold their ground
their identities forgotten
but featureless they stand
for the elements of man.

The Mozzie, 2005

Kalbarri National Park

The yellow sand road corrugates
"no camping, no dogs, no fires
undercut cliff edges, carry water".
Black scat glistens on ochre slabs.

Red playing cards tossed down
scooped up and spread apart
the Tumblagood sandstone sheared
layered and eroded into crawl caves.

We stand on a rib of rock
looped by the unlinked pools
of the Murchison, and look down
from humpy scrub to red river-gums.

The gorge engulfs. From crevices
Aron Ralston's dead arm beckons
but we keep to the track, like ants
on the concrete block of the barbeque site.

Famous Reporter, 2006

Mount Wellington

The riddling streams
and padding moss
gift packing them, are giving out.

The ferns are stiff
not loving, scratching
not flopping water down your neck.

It's summer.
She holds on.
The earth goes round in circles.

Quadrant, 2002
and as "Mt. Wellington in Summer", *The Mozzie*, 2006

Derwent estuary

On a glass morning
water fills the gaps between the rocks
pauses, drains
and comes up again
from underneath. Noiselessly.

On a glass morning
I am grateful
for the stillness
and the rise and fall of water in the rocks.

Studio, 2004

Golden boy

Even the exceptional die
Murray Rose is dead.
The nation mourns and his friends cry
Even the exceptional die.
An Olympic champion and nice guy
Our greatest male swimmer it is said.
Even the exceptional die
Murray Rose is dead.

Quadrant, 2013

Piltdown Man

I was seven when the Piltdown Man was shown to
    be a hoax
It was talked about at school and by many book-
    learned folks.

Biology teachers were incensed by the dishonesty
I didn't notice that, I was charmed by the audacity

The fooling of everyone, experts in particular
Arguments, the fragile reputations and the
    glamour.

The skull and the jaw were from different species
Only an inside man could have fitted such pieces.

I'd pull such a trick in a flash, given the
    wherewithal.
What's that say about me? I'd like to pay the world
    back is all.

Quadrant, 2012

Business

> Gina Rinehart and the kids
> are on page one
> and it's none of my business.

Quadrant, 2012

Bite the hand

> They had Nigella Bites being
> man-handled by her hubbie
> on Q and A the other day.
>
> Richo said he was a grub
> like a crow eating road-kill
> with a big smile on his mug
>
> and the person with the eye
> phone got pinned
> for not saving the world when he (she?) had
>   the chance.

Quadrant, 2014

The Spelling Police

Generations back
they invented
the IQ test

brought it to school
and took our brains'
finger-prints.

Predictably
the Spelling Police
came back for me.

But
I saw them first
and nicked off home.

Quadrant, 2003

Dyslexia
(for Betty Smith)

It looks like fields of gerberas.
There're kids with armfuls, meandering
– some pulling petals off
tossing, juggling, standing underneath
– going all gooey when the colours land upon their
    heads.

Lots hardly look side-ways, though
just walk along the snakes and ladders path
slightly bored and thinking
of the atom, one step down
the circuits in their brains making road maps of the
    maze.

But some unsuspecting little
more than toddlers
excited by the party, come running
full pelt, into razor wire
around fields of blackberries … that never die.

The pickers mock
The thorns hurt – they hold, they stop.
The teacher sools the pickers on
– it makes Mum and Dad sad.
One day one will write a poem that says,
    Fuck School.

Success Stories, 1999

The best days   of your life

If you couldn't
Spel
you weren't
just
in deep shit
you weren't
human.
Punishment   was being sat
                    on the gerls side
                    of the room.

"No more pencils
no more books
no more teachers
          ugly looks"
we sang
on break up day

the only way
out
before   Spell Check

Success Stories, 1999

Common psychiatrist

You want your mental illness treated
– because it's frightening and dangerous
You want an advocate on hand
– in anticipation of lack of sensitivity
 (but I am not empowered to take offence)
You want me keeping up to date
– while you're at films and barbeques
You want me charged
– for putting you in hospital against your will
You want me charged
– for not putting you in hospital against your will
You want the Coroner to screw me
– when I believe, when you tell me lies
You want me to be expensively insured
 (without passing on the cost to you)
– so you get buckets when you sue
You want for me, a fraction of the surgeon's fee
– for I can't do what they can do.

Australasian Psychiatry, 1997

Catatonia

We went to school together. Now
she's my patient, most of the time. Mute
staring and afraid. Madness spinning
behind once pretty eyes.

She strains to speak
I lean
but always
at the orgasmic moment, she stops.

So it goes
till I can stand no more
and give her ECT, against her will.
And we are free, for a week, maybe.

Quadrant, 1996

Friday's poem

Treed by work
– driven back and back
by consumers' rights
and not enough resources

with only desiccating caution
– dotting i's and crossing t's
to protect you.
Stiff as a board, Friday night

is poem writing time
– a quiver of pleasure at uncurling, not to mention
apprehension – lest you've gone too far, this time
and cannot be undone.

On the way, the chiropractor
straightens out
the working back
and at home, poem-birth sets the soul free.

Quadrant, 1996

Cheating at poetry

She pays a price I wouldn't be
prepared to pay, for poetry
or even science and humanity.

Nor is she, but she doesn't get
to pick. Her thoughts
written down, rush upon the reader

with a sweet ferocity we
can only read. She too
would rather not be basted

in madness, the reluctant central figure
of an occult horror film, co-starring
plotting worms and abusive shouting cows.

I get rejection slips, she gets none
for her work is never posted
and I am just as pleased. And justified:

madness is cheating when it comes to poetry.

Quadrant, 2000

Skulduggery

She comes with nits and lung
infection from no fixed address
hearing voices,
scared of churches
and asking to be killed.

The asylum was closed down
to set her free
from despots giving care
but she's begging to go back.

The persons in the counting
house can not believe their luck
free is cost effective:
better still,
it's central to the policy.

The Mozzie, 2005

Brilliance

I was injected, today
with a radioactive isotope
which attaches in the brain
to nerve endings
where thoughts are chemical quantities.

After a life-time of trying
to make a good impression, going straight,
like a drug addict I buzzed
with satisfaction, knowing
my ideas were brilliant (on the screen).

Quadrant, 1997

The two times table

Like a well flogged back
you never lose
the two times table
scar tissue, in brain cells of memory.

Post Vietnam
you're supposed to be "putting it on".
When you relive tripping on a mate's intestines
scream back, "Can you forget the two times table?"

Studio, 2004

A chance in hell

We didn't have a chance in hell
of choosing the right job –
we didn't have a clue
about the world, much less ourselves.

One teacher tried to warn kids
not to teach –
we thought he was unwell
and many trained and taught, in spite.

Dux meant medicine, and
good at maths was engineering –
there was no such job as poet. Anyway
the training's an endured life and a chance in hell.

Studio, 1997

Sagging

We went into her room
and there she was
hanged.
A belt
around her neck
and over a door handle.
We'd known she wanted out
but not how much.
Legs flat
on the floor
her backside one inch off
she'd sagged herself to death.

With face swollen and purple
And tongue too fat for
Her mouth
Sticking out
Like a Maori carving
And as dead as a lump of wood.

Too late for her and us. Now
for the recriminations
family anger
our own guilt
accusations of negligence, cover
ducking, state of the art scape-goating.

Off to the Coroner's court for questions
from a man who's never touched
a body.
Never
tried to help someone who wanted
to escape so much, she'd sag herself to death.

Quadrant, 1998

The policy

I'm a disappointment officer.
We all are
where I work
for the government resource-free
Health Department.
We're employed to implement
the policy of helping people
understand, they don't meet our criteria.

Overland, 2003

Tommy rot
(for Tom O'Byrne)

I am the man
who will only be buried
by men wearing leather-soled shoes.
They're hard to find, so

I'll be on the nose
but, it's all in my will
and they'll need an injunction
to get me into the ground.

I don't dislike progress
or animals either
(I prefer gumboots myself)
– but I'll be remembered

where others won't
as the man
who would only be buried
by men wearing leather-soled shoes.

Studio, 1997

In need of change

They changed the rules half way.
When I started, success
was respect.
Nurses stood
when the doctor
came into the office
– the doctor was embarrassed
but that was the way it was.
And authority
– what the doctor said
went.

The world is fairer now
egalitarian
with more rights
and transparency.

The top doctor spends her time
answering
valued complaints
and the bureaucrats decide
how many days
Grandma can have in hospital.

Quadrant, 2000

A Kosciuszko man applies himself

Ushered in, I shake hands with nine
well positioned people whose names
fly like chips in a chopping contest.
The long table resembling the deck of Noah's ark
with one of every kind around the edge.

In a team effort, prior to the ushering
they decided on the questions and
the answers that they simply had to hear.
But as a trying-out non-member
– I only got the questions.

They took my answers seriously
– at least none laughed.
But none smiled either
and I needed that nodding, smiling stuff
like chooks with a handful of wheat
– lots of heads going up and down and
a deal of contented clucking. That
didn't happen.

I've reached my peak.
Forget Everest, I'm a Kosciuszko man.

FreeXpresSion, 2001

Influence

This episode of illness starts unremarkably
apparently refreshed, your voices shout
some new insults into your ears, out
to the sides grey people move, to whip
away, when you try confronting them.
I increase your medication.

The trajectory goes wrong. You're not
as sad as you should be, in the face
of voices. I do your bloods again.
Another scan shows fine grained
something, of important insignificance.
Then you explain, you're having an affair.

Australasian Psychiatry, 2004

A day in Washington, DC

In a hotel room
in Washington, DC
away
from the decisions
that blemish
– things are pretty good.

There's air conditioning
room service
complimentary news papers
and a lift to save your legs.

I don't want
to reach into the past, that barbed-wire ball
papered over by distance and diversion
to fumble for a non-existent answer
to succeed, only
in churning up this blessed, becalmed day.

But one must always
be striving
not sitting, soaking up
not just enjoying
the pleasures of a propped clutch day.

So back we go to the subway of the mind
leaving serenity
for the land of opposition
– where health costs are contained
by the pain that can be born
but where, when a man murders
thirty-five
they gladly pay for thirty-five autopsies
in case it was only thirty-four, and one died of
    fright
– they wouldn't want to be unjust.

Back to where my job
is saying "no"
to those who want a "yes".

I waste the day
without finding
the non-existent answer (surprise)
but give myself the consolation prize
– the resolution
to never waste another hour on the search.

Studio, 1998

A transparency of doers

I was beavering away, but
as a sensible precaution, keeping
head well down, so
it came as quite a shock, when
the sniper fire of progress took me out.

At first I thought they got me through the brain
and I was dead. But on stress leave
– field hospital at home
I reassess and find, well sure, I'm dead
but we won't eat
if I don't keep
turning up till fifty-five
the superannuation rules are crystal clear.

As I speak, there are more inspectors
assessors, reviewers and investigators
of complaints
than we have shop floor doers.
It's all about transparency
– the doers who are left are X-rayed every day.

The question is to go or not to go, right now
on principle.
I'm not one for Eastern religion, but
I've got a wife and little boy, and
if Ghandi could see his way
to live to nearly eighty, why not me?

Quadrant, 2000

New secure psychiatric unit

It's really very nice
they've done a lovely job
in the space available.

Clean as a new pin
in speckled grey and green
the plaster dust and red flex swept

as far as the door
on the last day by leg-pulling
men with echoing radios.

Ten secure rooms
with no hanging points
as far as we can tell.

Ready for the voices
the conviction of delusion
the striking out in fear

the new futures
angry spouses
and the weeping parents.

The complaints of the advocates and
the watching waiting Boards
the Opposition, Ombudsman and Coroner

about the position of the taps
and the standard of our care. Today
we are thinking only, they've done a lovely job.

Quadrant, 2002

Coroner's delight

Another patient hung himself
in our ward today.
On a towel rail, this time.
Someone will have to pay.

The towel rail specifications
were for non-weight bearing
but this one bore sufficiently
for a suffocating death.

With any luck
they'll blame the builder.
His distress should do. And
lucky us, he doesn't work here anymore.

Australasian Psychiatry, 2002

Telemedicine

"Good morning, Mrs Smith.
This may seem a little strange at first
but if you will look into the camera
above the picture of my face
we can talk about your problems
just the same as I was there."

Well, I can't smell
you've had an accident
or even had a wash, of course
a reassuring touch of hand is out.

But, I can't be hauled before the Council
for touching you too much
and that's got to be a plus
for both of us.

Let's rewrite reality in images
shrink distance to the thickness
of a screen. Let's have
a TV personality for doctor
avoid the risk of being touched
by hand, and flesh-out the meaning of remote.

Australasian Psychiatry, 2002

Poetry reading

I don't have anything against poetry
or editors.
It's the public that pisses me off
they don't buy it.

There are some who can't not write the stuff
poor buggers.
And others say they write only for themselves
I don't buy that.

Surely everyone writes to be heard
poets included.
And this new electronic media is no way
the saviour.

Nothing is less suited to the ice screen
than poetry.
Then rap is the new poetry, perhaps?
That's crap.

Poetry is what it always was, it just doesn't
rhyme as much
and poets must just accept what comes
their way.

Long after Greece has left the Euro
Zone
and all the spin-doctors have been shot
for murder

the people will rise up and start reading poetry
again
and I will curse them from my grave for their
lousy timing.

Quadrant, 2013

A man sitting alone

The bolt slides snug
in the breech –
muffled by grease

locking brass and copper capsules
in front
of a compressed spring.

He thinks
and opts
for one by mouth.

Quadrant, 1997

Court appearances

There's nothing you can do.
Like all of us
she has to work
with the cards she got.

Her honesty gene is recessive
and the one she got
for impulse control
has never worked well.

She's as guilty
as hell
of getting
a poor hand at the deal.

Sidewalk, 2002

Think of a number

At seventeen
the bone rings of her neck were broken
and her cord custard was sheared
through
not all the way through.

Her body's hanging by a thread
so to speak, she can walk
like a puppet.

At seventeen
she worked after school in a fashion shop
had the gear and read the glossy mags
through
not all the way through.

She hasn't been outside since
"I don't want the people I knew
to see me."

At seventeen
she watched TV. Things haven't changed
except, she did forgive the driver
though
not all the way through.

It's time to tick the compensation box
but no one knows
what she's worth.

Famous Reporter, 2006

Medical Director

They held my nose and poured wet concrete
in my mouth. It filled my feet
legs and trunk, spilled over into fingers
arms, and finally my head.
But I wasn't dead, just concreted.

It wasn't rape. It was advertised and I applied
and gave my referees a call.
The job description didn't hint
at concrete treatments, and while a risk
I was vain and thought I could resist.

And I might have done in one on one, but
I hadn't reckoned on the main task, lying
to the Minister. So she believed what
she said, what was best for her politically.
You can get a taste for it apparently, not me.

Famous Reporter, 2004

Taking stock

I started at the edges of my mind sweeping my
    original thoughts
into an ankle-high pile in the middle.

Mostly they were dusty dry particles that billowed
When pushed too fast by the broom, with some
    special white ones
Like salt crystal and some even more promising
    bigger ones
Sparkling like grains of sugar.

A dust pan in one hand and a kitchen strainer in
    the other
I dug the pan under and fork lifted my ideas
Into the strainer, making sure to get every last one.
They rushed through as spray, desperate to be
    away.

One white theory lump, ideas that held together
    stopped.
Cautiously I picked it up between finger and thumb
But the connections were weak, and it shattered
into single grains which rouletted around and out
    through holes.

I'd love to have an original through the size
and durability of an al dente piece of macaroni.

Eureka Street, 2015

C. Chaplin: Retirement Counsellor

"In the end, life is a gag"
Said the indelible
Sir Charles Spencer Chaplin.
He amused me when I first heard him.

Said the indelible
Knight of the Realm at the top of his form
It amused me when I first heard it.
But it lost its charm when retirement winked.

All very fine at the top of one's form.
While trying to prove that my life had mattered
It lost its charm as retirement winked.
Then I saw the blighter was right!

While hoping to prove that my life had mattered
I resisted that silly old Charles Spencer Chaplin.
But of course the bastard was right
"In the end, life is a gag."

Quadrant, 2015

A sort of reunion

I've saw you before.
Your father uster have the Ampol
Petrol station in Cunnamulla.

But you didden do your schoolun here
you went across to Brissie
for your schoolun, from early on.

And now you're back as the doctor?
Well, goodness me.
We need more men on the Fire Brigade?

Idiom, 2016

Sunbaking

The sea breathes
slowly sucking in
pausing
then letting go with a thump
and a tinkle at the edge.
The sun pulses
pushing warm narcotic
through the back
to the core.

Christians Writing, 1986

Granny-knots

Back in Cubs
knots were important:
bowline, sheepshank and clovehitch.

The reef-knot was the touchstone
flat and symmetrical
never mistaken by old hands
for the lumpy granny-knot.

Some never learned
and others lost
those childhood secrets.
But their kids' tents
still withstand storms
thanks to granny-knots.

Studio, 1994

Good puddles

There aren't the puddles
there used to be, for kids
to draw them in
sliding feet, not stepping
– a funny feeling on the instep
then around the ankle, and further up.

Till the top
of the gumboot wobbles –
at which point
even saying sorry
(to God)
or backing off, is perilous

when luck decides
if thin sides hold
the dam curve back
or buckle and fold in
dropping dumps of water onto socks –
instructing on risks and consequences.

On Being Alive, 1997

The message of Christmas

You buy the best, lots of it
there's heaps left over
on Boxing Day and through
to New Year's Day
(when the second swag arrives).

You live on surplus
smoked salmon and macadamia nuts
till you're sick of it
and long for a normal meal.

The message of Christmas
– go easy on yourself.
Even if you cracked it
you couldn't hack the high life.

Quadrant, 1996

Life as diversion therapy

This boy looked
over the rejection of childhood
to the fat years of autonomy
kept his head down
and pedalled determination
through the best years of kids' lives.

He got a job
running up
escalators going down
near the top
he tired to a walk
and was carried back
to the beginning.

"You can't escape," said the sand
of time, and the old man didn't mind.

Centoria, 1997

Elephant

I bought an antique piece
of elephant hide
– cut to the shape
of Ceylon
– faced with an ivory map.

You are not dead, Dear Elephant.
Your liver was eaten
by a worm, that nourished
a bush, that gave the tea
my mother drank.
It helped her womb grow.

The ashes of your bones
blew out to sea
and were eaten by a fish
that was eaten by a shark
that was eaten by my father
and made his back strong.

Your heart was eaten
by a rat, that was eaten
by a maggot, that became
a tree, that became
a stamp, that I collected
and it made me think.

Great and Wonderful Elephant
you are not forgotten.
Do not grieve
my cruel ornament.
It reminds me
of the molecules I owe to you.

Island, 1998

A possible sighting

Threatening walls thump
shells and crab claws
into sand, to be carried
into oysters, to make pearls.
Along the beach, on the rocks

a fish with silver scales
(alive, courtesy of the sun
– ninety million miles away)
is caught on a line by a girl
who thought she caught a glimpse of God.

Studio, 2001

Shelling

A cockle,
halves locking
as a carapace, is washed up.

A child,
walking, finding
this sarcophagus, picks it up.

The acquisition
of armour
by innocents, is growing up.

Island, 1996

A boy from school

I remember the face
Of a boy from school
Who was lost in the bush and never found.

I always see him crying for his mother.
But he's ahead now
His dying is behind him.

Quadrant, 2013

An eye to the future

When I was a boy I saw
a world
of cigarette cases and rowing boats
and I could hardly wait.

But the owners died
before I could take over
and the people just ahead
took it down, like an outside lavatory.

Now my son thinks
he'll get a job
and be able
to pick his nose on the telephone.

Quadrant, 1996

Whaling

We are whales
trailing rope
from bent harpoons
rusted thin over time.

The barbs hold
firm in flesh
as water washes
pus holes clean.

Side by side
in trust we fear
one more wound
will kill us.

LiNQ, 1991

Having your go

I didn't know I was on.
I kept waiting
for the man to start my turn.

All of a sudden
he took me off
and said my go was over.

I can tell those who don't know.
I cup my hands and shout into the wind
"You're having your go."

Quadrant, 1993

Offering

I will tell you how it feels
to be past your prime

I will tell you all I know
if I know you're listening.

Tirra Lirra, 2005

A man watching

A broken necklace
a row of beads
a long limp string
dangling on a public bench

near the water. Ripples
before the waves of the day
come, between when the sun rises
and the need to shield your eyes.

Where wooden dinghies bumped
– now aluminium bongs.
A man avoided happiness
for fear of losing

and knowing what he'd lost
– as dull days slip
drop with the gravity of time
and sink in the estuary of his life.

Red Jelly, 1994

Nations Earth Summit II

In the days when
the jug blew, you fixed it
– adventure was something you left home to do.

The jug blew this week
I couldn't buy an element
                      "well, they're a sealed unit."

I went home
for an adventure
on the Internet, of interactive pornography.

Jugs are sealed
genitalia are revealed
– welcome to economic rationalism.

Don't interfere.
Paternalism is out
– it's immoral to tamper with market forces.

It's economic suicide
– greenhouse gas emission limits.
I don't give a bugger much about myself

– it's my son I care about
– but he'll be the same. For his happiness
I need to love his children, whom I will never see.

Home Brew, 1999

October 28

The sun, down below the hills
still somehow brushes the hulls
of moored pleasure boats. The birds,
after their pre-dusk flurry
hush. Muted happiness called
contentment binds and
I want to live forever.

It would've been easy years ago
when the struggle was so bloody
hard, and we gave death her chance.
Now, the unknown mischievous God
gets his/her own back.
If you want to stay, you can't.

Famous Reporter, 1993

Waiting for the day

Like mice at night
clumsy moves and heavy tackles
of thirty years ago
come back to sup at joints
shoulder, neck and knees.

The decisions of the day
are examined grain by grain
for hairline chinks
which could let the lawyers in
to take the house and all.

Mouth dry and bladder full
I give up hope, pretence
of sleep, rustle into clothes
quietly, to protect the wife
and go to watch the dawn.

A rope loops, the waking water
crinkles at the edge
a grey pink transition time
a deceitful, treasured time
a time when other people don't exist.

Quadrant, 1993

Inflation

I was on the ropes, thinking
while their blows, no longer painful
but a worry all the same
dabbed at that energy
without which one is old

and the bell clanged for a rest.

Something wasn't working right
and when it rang
to come out of the corner
my sitting legs had given up
and wouldn't take me to the fight.

So, they all stood over me
City Hall included
flinging down last rites
– till you arrived, with the kiss of life
like a bicycle pump
and they pulled back as we inflate.

Quadrant, 1994

The Birthday Girl

She's the Birthday Girl
at fifty-two, she's ten years old
for one
more
day.

At first light, presents from the family
in the afternoon
the celebrated jewel, in a circle of the girls.

A happy life
the waiter thinks – The Lucky Thing!
What does he know
of the ambush
– of the crab within her breast.

Centoria, 2000

Rubbing out

Before we knew a rubber was a franger in
 American
we had the real thing. Not
these white and transparent
poly-something ones, of the sixties and thereafter.

Before pollution, when erasers were just rubber
things got pretty grubby. Hands
had to get inspected and
the chattels of your desk got black with lead.

Our rubbers cracked and crumbled in their
 perishing
but the rich kids' ones went worse
and got sticky. We faced the hero's choice
– stay with your mistake or take the chance

for rubbing out could make a bigger mess.
No back-space key
– there was polio and cane
you got either, none or both

but for things that you could change
you had to hold on long
enough, to go down through the layers
– the remedial smudge before the mark, to a nice
 white beginning.

Island, 2001

Can't buy me love

Watch out for nightmares
on ulcer medicine. Heads
with jaws smashed. Dogs
eating human tongues. And
you can't swallow.

All you want is pay your taxes
private health insurance, live
a quiet life, close
to services, avoid
the horror of triggers
the triggers of horror.

Does ulcer medicine make horror
or just release what is already there?
Who is this man I'm living in?

Studio, 2002

Growing old

You don't want everything
anymore.

Having the best-looking woman
around
is no longer an imperative
and the thought of making love
to a taut
thirty-year-old adolescent
is as welcome as losing your keys.

If you're not the boss
you feel sorry
for him
about to be retired
from the power that meant so much.

And there's nothing
like an old enemy
walking toward you on the footpath.
You find
you're free
of the glowing coal of hate
that's been burning in your chest
since school.

Now there's the bond
of soldiers
who've stood toe
to toe
against a common foe.

You balance the arthritis with the ease of age.

Quadrant, 1995

Swaps

Christopher Robin
complained till he died
of the fame
father foisted
upon him –

which Clinton
fired missiles to gain.
Would the people who want
to be somebody else
please, now, swap places.

Quadrant, 1998

Sail

Cut to a pattern
nailed to the mast
and boom
I'm flat
and tight as a ping
to a finger flick.

A breeze quivers
a hand pulls
the rudder angles
and I am pregnant with the wind.
The wood is groaning
and the people are happy

until I rip
top to bottom
and flap in their faces.

Quadrant, 2003

Jealous of a visual artist

You never give a thought to things
that bother me. Superannuation
kissing arse just right and
keeping the lawn mower quiet.

When you need wine, rent
(you never plan ahead)
you take a minute off
from carousing, laughing, eating
(you live simultaneously)
to paint a picture
of intelligence and beauty
for a quick buck. Then back to life you go.

Studio, 1995

A few days to yourself

Don't make me sit
on a perfect beach
the sun strained through the trees
and one evening gull
landing
where the things I've done
can come for me.

Leave me shortfalls
overruns and strikes
as trees against the sun.

Siglo, 1995

Losing his marbles

He misplaced the present
but rummaged, till
another marble slipped his mind
and he lost
his past as well, in free fall future.

Australasian Psychiatry, 1993

Packaging

This young bloke turned eighteen
they don't have twenty-first
majority, the way we did.

He's got everything
that has ever been invented
a computer and a battery operated watch.

I gave him a paper dictionary
– in retrospect
it should have been on CD ROM.

But the words would be OK
a little out of date perhaps
– I didn't check for "nerds" or "byte"

but by and large there'd be enough
for pleasure and protection.
They're not mine to give of course

I just paid for the packaging.

Sidewalk, 2000

Three shells

I found them on a stall
unexpectedly (I'd given up
on reading books
collecting stamps – things made by men)
three shells from the sea.

Indian Ocean, probably.
One blown-glass thin, two
heavy in the hand like tusk
– sad bastions
with ghosts only to protect.

One spherical, one flat and
one a spike
– the colours bright.
There for me
to come across, and wonder at the sea.

Famous Reporter, 2001

Making a will

Please, leave everything in order.

Just put down how much
you love each person
match with your responsibilities
(load scores for blood, adoptive status
and each one's prospects
for making their own way)
cover all eventualities
check it for morality
on a piece of A4 paper.

Just bang it down
in legalese, if you please.
This is final
the most important statement of your life.

No, you can't put kisses at the bottom
that's the mark
of someone who can't write.

Mattoid, 1997

Beyond the drive-in

The drive-in is forgotten
by the generation it conceived
– never held its grandchildren
and was never mourned

for technology has no track
for tradition, and the consumer
is too drunk on change. Going
to the next phase, pay TV

and the information super highway
will close the corner video shop
and like hypochondriacs, we'll fake malfunctions
for human contact with the service man.

Island, 1997

Pinching bottles

Back in the fifties
sixpence (a zac)
was a lot of money to a kid.

You used to get tuppence back
on little soft-drink bottles
and sixpence
on the big ones.
If you found a little bottle
you were pretty happy
and went to the shop
for some lollies.
You could get two one penny lollies
like Clinkers or Cobbers
or a lot of cheap ones.
Licorice Squares were good
you got four for a penny
and they lasted.
Rainbow Balls used to be good too.
They used to come in different colours
and go white
when you sucked the colour off.
I remember when they changed
Rainbow Balls from
four a penny to two a penny.
Eta peanuts used to come in
little red and yellow grease-proof paper packets.
They were threepence a packet
and came in big square, silver tins
with round lids.

You always used to get cheap lollies
Unless you found a big bottle
and then you might get
one of the expensive ones
(Cobbers were the best out of them
because they lasted the longest).
You only got a packet of peanuts
when your uncle bought them for you.
You would chew each half separately
to mush
to make them last.
The salt was the best part
it was different to the salt you had at home.
Rich kids
when Coke was fivepence 'to drink there'
when they found a big bottle
they would get a bottle of Coke
to drink there, and one Clinker.
But we didn't get drinks 'to drink there'.
That only lasted as long as you were in the shop
and the man would be there, waiting
and you would have to hurry up
and you had no privacy.
We used to get away by ourselves
with a bag of lollies
and savour
every sweet second.
The quantity of seconds
rather than the quality of the sweetness
was the critical factor.
Anyway
I found a gold-mine.

About half a mile away
from our place was a bowling club
and I discovered
that every Sunday morning
there was a big bottle
out on their back steps.
You had to climb a five-foot fence
to get it.
I used to feel guilty
but the temptation was too great.
We all have our price –
mine used to be sixpence
– I wonder what it is now?

Studio, 1997

The love of science
(for Mary)

Like other men, he cuts back
gets himself committee free
plans camping trips
and more time with the kids.

Makes his goal the mortgage
the here and now. Till
an idea, that just might work
slips beneath his guard

and he gets the rush, again.
The tumbling thoughts, rapid
talk, the quick movements of a feeding bird
the excitement, the race

the gamble, the shot at fame
the thrill of being first.
Closed brain loops, buzz
break, and spiral out, recruiting

grey cells by the scoopful.
The atom bomb, once billowing
can't be contained by a single, crucible
skull. Then

the drudgery of proof – for fools.
Of getting grants
of the opinions, of brain-dead referees
who wouldn't have a clue. The pushing

on, the late nights and details.
The kids' hockey matches missed.
The disappointment
of the step that wouldn't work. The despair.

The withdrawal.
The same new resolutions, the turning back
to the family, to find
they left, last month, with a brickie's mate.

Blast, 1997

High tide

At high tide, in the morning
the waves stop
to ruminate
with the water full
up
under
long legged jetties
swallowed down
to be easily heaved
and tossed as puny sticks
on a broad back
from below the curve
brooding.

We sacrifice our lives
on dedicated slabs of time
await each turning of the tide
and never know how close we came.

Famous Reporter, 1997

Congratulatory poem
(for Les Murray)

At a shack, at night
going for a pee
it's as cold as a witch's tit
and I trip.
Age, a parasite
is sucking from my bones
where they come together
in rusted joints

while Les A. Murray's
on a German junket
going for a gong –
the Petrarch prize –
being fabled and flattered
that night.

And in a computerless school
in a stranded place
plays a child who knows
intuitively, of energy and matter
government and Mozart
and the world waits
unaware, for the outcome
of choice and the fall of the cards.

Studio, 1997

Suffrage

Must remember – vote
tomorrow
or cop a fine.

I couldn't name the Shadow Minister
for Education or the Minister
for Sport and Recreation, for that matter.

I can tell you zip about – the Democrats
on Mabo – I know naught
of the Nationals' policy on science.

And to a Greenie
is a whale more important than a tree?
Search me.

I'm a blind man with a gun
tomorrow
I fire – that's the law.

At least
if someone's hurt
they can't blame me – it's a secret ballot.

Home Brew, 1998

Business as usual

Kitted out by sleep. Ready
for a hard nosed day's
head kicking, toe cutting.
Eyes on the ball
the big picture is
there's always room at the top.

A tickle
like a hair in the throat.
Try to get it with finger and thumb
miss it. Swallow
try to ignore. But it catches again.
Huff it up and this time grab

the memory of the girl
last night
crying
over her dead grandfather
and friend.
Her salty kiss.

Forgotten
the child's loss
overshadowed
by lust
for the market kill
– expunged by one night's sleep.

Studio, 1999

Painting

It's a lump inside her head
a foetus kicking out
her sleep contracts
she gets up in pain.

First stage, she doodles
clicks her tongue
slaps her pencil down
and walks off angry.

One night, at half past ten
she paints a canvas white
and goes to bed.
This time she sleeps.

Morning lead lines never stand a chance
going under to the colour
– from the blank vagina
comes her child alive.

LiNQ, 2001

The missing helicopter

Back when a copper stick was made of wood
and we sat up to ice-cream from a cardboard box
you'd tell us how our lives were going to be.

Every house would have a telephone
inside, the part you talk into
no, not the red box too.

Every wireless would have a face
like a cocky in a cage
no, you wouldn't have to clean it out.

Men would fly up to the Moon
and jump like kangaroos
no, they wouldn't grow a tail.

Mum, you were absolutely right
in everything you said. But quick
before you die, where's my helicopter?

Wellspring, 2001

The triple-jump in contemporary Australia

The skateboard came
thirty years ago
– I'm waiting for the craze to pass.

Baggy pants, crew cuts, caps on back to front
they ski without snow
surf without waves
slalom between pedestrians
leaving them to grumble to the papers.

Men from Mad Max
they come
on rumbling wheels
dull first, then roaring
packs in a pre-petrol phase.

Ear-rings in their eyebrows
they come
the roaring at its peak
they sweep between
a brief-case is sent spilling.

They pass, the roaring drops.
They leap
as athletes
acrobats, their boards obey
– astronauts in weightlessness
above the gutter

then whizz across the crown and jump
up, onto
the footpath on the other side.

The grass is gone
the track is now high-tech
Teflon sort of stuff
and the triple-jump is dead.
Time to embrace the ballet of the streets.

Alive Magazine, 1999

Science of fantasy

Sub-atomic particles
fired across a CRO
hit the screen
and show me Donald Duck.

I've never seen an atom
but I have seen Donald Duck.
Science versus fantasy.
Forget the quarks, I believe in ducks.

The Mozzie, 2006

Pretty day

Birds, black spots on finials spat
into a horizontal grey morning
Spit-fire swoop beneath
wires, as freighter pigeons climb.

No one wants this bit of day
before the cars get up
a front door bangs, a sculpted dog
comes out to foul the footpath.

Gripped pens authorize the lost
and found, the other woman's ring
beneath the back seat of deceit
and school fees due this week.

Church bells clang to press
the guilt of those who will not come
and end a day bent into war
by love or hate and vanity.

Spindrift, 2000

To understand the universe

The orbit of the earth is straight.
It seems to be a circle
because time is bent by bodies

and, when a star runs out of puff
it becomes a 'white dwarf'
or space-vacuuming black hole.

We know, courtesy of Heisenberg's
uncertainty and 'imaginary
numbers' (which are negative when squared)

that, the universe is finite
but without an edge!

Can we be talking circular

with no beginning, sides or end?
The Aranda tribe was talking
of the eternal Now of Dreamtime

before the crucifixion
– when a hole dug in the sand
became our point for counting time.

Island, 2001

Seven Mile Beach

It gets harder
to get your wet suit on

One day it won't be worth it
and you'll have to be content

with hot dry sand on bare feet
shards of shell

glare on waves, their
thump and expiring foam

perfect white gulls, in spite
of their scraping call

and the sea breeze
rubbing over your ears

And you **will** be:
you're still getting ready.

Valley Micropress, 2006

Telegram boys

Before telephones in homes
lived the tribe of telegram boys.
With pouches on belts they rode red bikes.
When Mum died, off to the Post Office
to pick your words at a shilling apiece
prepositions were a waste.
On the minimum charge you might get
"One more word …" for nothing and add Love.

Then suits came out with telephones in the pockets
telegram boys were oral history and everyone could talk.
Until text messages arrived.
Now writing's back, in letters telegram boys can't read.
Their bodies rusted beyond riding
they listen for the returning spoken word.

Island, 2005

The pencil sharpener

It's a bit disconcerting, the pencil fits in snugly
But sticks out at an angle to the housing.
You check and reassured start twisting gently
Wood thinner than women's underwear crawls
    over your fingers
And as long as there are no jerks or withdrawals
It continues a virgin ribbon.
The lead is shaved of powder to pin point tall
And the smell of Californian cedar is not forgotten.

It's all in the position
Of a tiny blade
In a confined space.
Completing the mission
For which it was made
A salute to the human race.

Quadrant, 2013

Friday afternoon

Four grades of glass paper
from coarse down to fine
four separate sheets
lying on a desk
flicking back light as points, here and there.

Four grades of glass paper
ready for the rubbing
to make wood dust
to make wood smooth
and liberate that smell you only get from trees.

Four grades of glass paper
lying on a desk
on a Friday afternoon
ready for the weekend
to Stargate the office guy to the realm of touch.

The Mozzie, 2006

Back garden

A brick walkway between stone houses
with corner moss and dark green bushes
causing cracks, leads to an overgrown
garden, where clinging things porridge over
fences. A small blue flower speaks up

plants can be identified, but the lighter green
of rapid growth has snookered order. An
un-pruned apple tree, blooming branches
to the grass, aniseed weed sticking up
grey, the only angles in a hip-high sea.

Starlings and honeyeaters perch, call and fly
confused. The dowdy lady living here was
garden proud. The tendril of a pokie
grabbed her wrist, and she couldn't twist
away. She doesn't bother with manure anymore.

Blue Dog, 2005

Platypus

Usually, you don't see
platypuses
just a flash and a splash in a billabong.
But this time one came
walking along the track.
He didn't seem to see us, just went past.

Apparently, they do that.
Decamp
and go off to find another stream
blind except for programming
not thinking through
what could happen, should they meet people on
    the way.

We thought he must be sick and scooped
him in a coat (they've got poison spurs one said)
and took him back to his cool
pool, to recover. But
we later learnt they can do that
just get out, and go to somewhere else.

He wasn't good at walking
kind of scratched along
the path on claws instead of feet.
He wasn't there
when we came back
we might have killed the little beast.

Tirra Lirra, 2005

Gulls

On Franklin Wharf we came across
a big Pacific gull
pulling at a bone

and standing off
a smaller silver gull
still, watching.

As we approached
(my boy to get a closer look)
the bigger bird backed off
and the smaller one
stepped up
and took the prize.

So we backed off
– the initial order was restored
we approached again, and again
– the pieces changed their places
as though connected, underground
by pulleys linked with string.

We scared them differentially.
We stood where the smaller gull could gorge
and the larger one would not impose
We screwed with natural selection – helping out the
    underdog
unaware, we were the smaller bird.

Studio, 2005

Windlass

With the wife away and Gulf War Two
the only show on radio
I get out
and walk along the rocks.

They've knocked down the next but one.
Brick pillars
a few foundations stand
a corner wall.

An arm-powered windlass, rusting
resting, after years
of pulling boats ashore
in a pile of junk.

Get a spanner, I bring it home
a conversation piece that worked
with a man attached
winding up the slack of human frailty.

The Mozzie, 2005

The face

Superficial muscles as orbicularis oculi and oris
procerus, zygomaticus major, zygomaticus minor
buccinator, corrugator supercilii, going down
to the muscles of mastication, the masseter
temporalis and the medial and lateral pterygoids.

The ophthalmic artery wriggles into infra- and
supra-orbital branches as the facial nerve splits
into zygomatic, mandibular and buccal branches
and the temporomandibular joint waits
beneath parotid gland, just before the ears.

Vena vorticosa, vitreous body and optic foramen
of the eye, and the stylohyoid and styloglossus
suspend the tongue from styloid processes
of the skull, the frontal, maxilla, sphenoid and
zygomatic bones. Beauty lies beneath the skin.

Studio, 2004

Shoes

Let me comfort you
We will never meet
But I know the pinch of your shoe.

You did the best you could do
And as we have the same feet
Let me comfort you.

Poof! Our time flew.
Nor could I ever get the beat.
But I know the pinch of your shoe.

Was it bad luck? Not a clue!
But, as you toss at stony sleep
Let me comfort you.

You never had a thought completely new
I never had a thought profoundly deep.
I do know the pinch of your shoe.

Not for us the prism of new dew.
This is not a secret that you keep.
Let me comfort you.
I too have the pinch of your shoe.

Quadrant, 2014

It got lost

What happened to the gold watch?
What happened to working in one place all
    your life?
Sometimes such things get lost.
What happened to all those blokes you worked
    with?

What happened to working in one place all
    your life?
Sometimes you only see things looking back.
What happened to those blokes you worked with?
And playing football for the team where you
    grew up?

Sometimes you only see things looking back
Like trachoma was a worry once.
If they can pay you can play where you grew up
But loyalty pays nobody's bills.

Trachoma was a worry once
And sometimes such things get lost.
But loyalty pays nobody's bills.
What happened to the gold watch? I sold it.

Quadrant, 2015

The Awá People

Three members of the pre-contact Awá tribe
Walked out of the Amazon jungle and when
Told about pollution, global warming and ISIS
They wanted to go back, but it was too late. They'd
Already been gifted a Coca-Cola and a bucket of
    KFC.

Vine Leaves Literary Journal, 2016

Nicking

If you nicked the Sydney Harbour Bridge
the mandatory sentence should be
– you have to keep it.

Because, where would you put it
– with land prices as they are?
That would stop bridge nicking for good.

Quadrant, 2014

The ring of bone
(for Arabella)

The ring of bone is fortress walls
warm pulsed not cold stone
holding hiding from worldly mauls
    The ring of bone.

Protecting minus time releasing with a groan
through the safety of the ring of bone come all
stay at home or sail the world of fame or foam
    The girdle of caul.

Unmarked ungiving not a single fall
until our mother's grave dirge moan
we put beneath her head a crocheted shawl.
    The ring of bone.

Idiom, 2014

as in cummings

For the sake of an 'e'
The word was wrong.

Moral is bad
When morale is good.

Quadrant, 2015

Things

There didn't seem much point to log books
after we got slide rules.
Now, there doesn't seem much point to surf boats
because of jet-skis.

But some people like old things
like throwing the javelin at the Olympics Games
even though at the next pavilion they're blasting
    away with Magnums.

There didn't seem much point to slide rules
after we got calculators.
Now there doesn't seem much point to milk bottles
because of cardboard cartons.

But some people like old things
like collecting Bakelite telephones
even though we now have better ones in our
    pockets.

There didn't seem much point to dedicated
    calculators
after we got computers.
Now there doesn't seem much point in knives and
    forks
because of Colonel Sanders.

But some people like old things
like the history of the British Empire
even though it's bad to be proud of what the
    colonialists did.

Australian Poetry Journal, 2015

A trip to the tip

We had a television for the tip
Old, heavy as a mountain, though still going.
But too bulky and it didn't fit
The space left by the new skirting.
With betrayal in my heart we trolleyed
It to the car, hearsed it off and
Paid ten dollars to the man employed
To take a good TV off your hands.

It was put down beside an orange witch's hat
Which was the only spot of gaiety that day.
The crows were undaunted by the tip cat
and sulky standing gulls had naught to say.
We live in fear of being replaced
By a slimmer one with a better face.

Eureka Street, 2015

Pithed

I'm pithed said the reed
I'm pithed said the helmet
I'm pithed said the frog
I'm pithed said the drunk
And they were all right.

Quadrant, 2016

Kepler-452b

It's a long way away, but it is there.

A telescope way out in the Cygnus constellation
Sent strings of zeros and ones, describing
    Kepler-452b.
It's a little further from its star than we are
But, theirs is a little hotter than ours.
It's in the Goldilocks zone, not too hot and not too
    cold.

It's a long way away, but it is there.

It's a bit bigger than Earth, so
The gravity will be about double. Not
Impossible but not the place for jogging.
Its atmosphere is twice as thick. An
Interesting feature, not a problem.

It's a long way away, but it is there.

It was a world without violence or weapons
Where the trees think and the cows vote (green).
Back home we prepared a colonising force, when
They sent a message. They'd been fooling around. If
We ever returned, they'd turn Earth into a
    cantaloupe.

Quadrant, 2015

What a time!

Carbon paper blue, black, red and green
And stamps, Olympians, trains and Queens
All here well before me.
I survived
Carbon paper, but stamps'll limp along

Long after I am gone.
I'm a soul brother of
White Out. I remember when that came in.
Now, it's getting hard to get, and I've
got this filial feeling we're going out together.

My grandfather saw cars come in.
And I saw computers
The biggest stride we've ever strode.
What a time in history!
I want to be buried in a 3D printed coffin.

Quadrant, 2015

Index to poems

1965	58
A boy from school	130
A chance in hell	103
A day in Washington, DC	110
A few days to yourself	146
After asthma	12
A Kosciuszko man applies himself	108
Ali Abbas	87
A man sitting alone	117
A man watching	134
An eye to the future	131
A possible sighting	129
Around the turn	16
as in cummings	178
A sort of reunion	123
A transparency of doers	112
A trip to the tip	180
Back garden	170
Back home	71
Before hockey	66
Beyond the drive-in	150
Bite the hand	93
Bradman played cricket	48
Brilliance	102
Bronte Hydro Village	73
Business	93
Business as usual	159
Call to table	3
Can't buy me love	141
Catatonia	98
Caught on the hop	45

C. Chaplin: Retirement Counsellor	122
Cheating at poetry	100
Child	8
Common psychiatrist	97
Congratulatory poem	157
Cordless in Mexico	24
Coroner's delight	114
Court appearances	118
Cradle Mountain and surrounds	83
Dachau	76
Dad	20
Dad 1	25
Day Two	2
Demolition of the Battery Point boat sheds	63
Derwent estuary	91
Descending stairs	19
Driving to Craigie Knowe Vineyard	70
Dyslexia	95
Elephant	128
Emma and the moth	5
Emma's dog	10
Father figure	14
Firdo Square	85
First teacher	4
Fish hooks	5
For sale	9
Frail	29
Friday afternoon	169
Friday's poem	99
Gameboy	13
Going overboard	44

Golden boy	91
Good puddles	125
Grandma	22
Granny-knots	124
Granny's place	3
Growing old	142
Gulls	172
Harrington Richardson	35
Having your go	133
Hawley Beach 1	59
Hawley Beach 2	68
Her rings	41
High tide	156
How television saved the world	74
Inflation	138
Influence	109
Informed consent	32
In need of change	107
It got lost	176
Jealous of a visual artist	145
Kaesong River, 1952	56
Kakadu	51
Kalbarri National Park	89
Kepler-452b	181
Kursk	77
Laurens Koster	67
Life as diversion therapy	127
Life's work	43
Limited edition	2
Living comet	30
Locked on	86

Losing his marbles	146
Love	37
Ludwig II	54
Madrid 2004	84
Making a will	149
Manneken Pis	65
Mary	49
McGrath	64
Medical Director	120
Mentioned in dispatches	55
Migraine	37
Mount Wellington	90
Nations Earth Summit II	135
New secure psychiatric unit	113
Nicking	177
Noel (3)	26
Noel (4)	27
NX5331	28
October 28	136
Offering	133
On a jetty	66
On the Maria Island ferry	62
Our psychotic cat	17
Out walking	21
Packaging	147
Painting	160
Piltdown Man	92
Pinching bottles	151
Pithed	180
Platypus	171
Poem to a woman	42

Poetry reading	116
Port Arthur	75
Preparing for the River Styx	31
Pretty day	164
Queenstown, Tasmania	72
Racing Emma	7
Reel	47
Rubbing out	140
Sagging	104
Sail	144
Saving Grandma's walker	23
Science of fantasy	163
Seven Mile Beach	166
Shed fire	15
Shelling	130
Shoes	175
Skulduggery	101
Snails	60
Split second	36
Suffrage	158
Sunbaking	123
Swaps	143
Taking down the Christmas tree	11
Taking stock	121
Telegram boys	167
Telemedicine	115
Thanks for the extra arm	38
The Awá People	177
The best days of your life	96
The Birthday Girl	139
The Boy's Own Annual	10

The brave tram driver	61
The Centre Pompidou	78
The counsellor is coming	46
The face	174
The fight of our lives	6
The Hiroshima of divorce	39
The Hon. R. A. Pargiter	57
The love of science	154
The McCord Museum	81
The message of Christmas	126
The missing helicopter	161
The old man	18
The pencil sharpener	168
The people of the *Batavia*	52
The Pinnacles	82
The policy	105
The ring of bone	178
The Spelling Police	94
The Story of the Bead People	50
The triple-jump in contemporary Australia	162
The two times table	102
Things	179
Thinking on death	69
Think of a number	119
Three shells	148
Tommy rot	106
To understand the universe	165
Us	20
Venezia	79
Victoria	80
Waiting for the day	137

Walking near Mt Fuji	88
Whaling	132
What a time!	182
What there is	1
Windlass	173
Winter	34
Work	86
Yellow dress	40

Index to publications

Alive Magazine : 162
Australasian Psychiatry : 19, 20, 54, 57, 97, 109, 114, 115, 146
Australian Poetry Journal : 179
Blast : 154
Blue Dog : 84, 170
Brave New Word : 39, 40, 44
Broad Seat : 38, 65, 76
Centoria : 3, 12, 71, 127, 139
Christians Writing : 123
Core : 73
Edgeways : 41
Eureka Street : 121, 180
Famous Reporter : 2, 31, 34, 50, 66 (2), 89, 119, 120, 136, 148, 156
FreeXpresSion : 21, 108
Fremantle Arts Review : 51
Gathering Force : 63
Home Brew : 5, 135, 158
Idiom : 23, 49, 58, 123, 178
Imago : 25, 52
Island : 128, 130, 140, 150, 165, 167
Lexicon : 62
LiNQ : 9, 132, 160
Mattoid : 14, 59, 68, 149
Muse : 32, 80
New England Review : 22
On Being Alive : 125
Overland : 105
Past the Poppies : 28, 64

Quadrant : 2, 10, 16, 18, 20, 24, 26, 27, 29, 30, 35, 36, 37 (2), 61, 72, 77, 78, 81, 82, 90, 91, 92, 93 (2), 94, 98, 99, 100, 102, 104, 107, 112, 113, 116, 117, 122, 126, 130, 131, 133, 137, 138, 142, 143, 144, 168, 175, 176, 177, 178, 180, 181, 182

Red Jelly : 134

Redoubt : 60

Sidewalk : 79, 118, 147

Siglo : 146

Spindrift : 15, 69, 164

Studio : 1, 5, 6, 7, 13, 17, 43, 45, 67, 70, 74, 75, 86, 91, 102, 103, 106, 110, 124, 129, 141, 145, 151, 157, 159, 172, 174

Success Stories : 95, 96

The Mozzie : 46, 47, 48, 55, 83, 85, 86, 87, 88, 90, 101, 163, 169, 173

Tirra Lirra : 133, 171

Valley Micropress : 166

Vine Leaves Literary Journal : 177

Visions : 10

Weekend Australian : 11

Wellspring : 3, 4, 8, 161

Westerly : 56

Writing : 42

www.ingramcontent.com/pod-product-compliance
Lightning Source LLC
Chambersburg PA
CBHW071217090426
42736CB00014B/2861